changing with the tides

also by shelby leigh

it starts like this: a collection of poetry

changing with the tides

shelby leigh

G

Gallery Books

New York   London   Toronto   Sydney   New Delhi

G

Gallery Books
An Imprint of Simon & Schuster, Inc.
1230 Avenue of the Americas
New York, NY 10020

This Gallery Books trade paperback edition July 2022

GALLERY BOOKS and colophon are registered trademarks
of Simon & Schuster, Inc.

For information about special discounts for bulk purchases, please
contact Simon & Schuster Special Sales at 1-866-506-1949
or business@simonandschuster.com.

The Simon & Schuster Speakers Bureau can bring authors to
your live event. For more information or to book an event, contact
the Simon & Schuster Speakers Bureau at 1-866-248-3049 or
visit our website at www.simonspeakers.com.

Interior design by Laura Levatino
Front and back cover by Islam Farid

Manufactured in the United States of America

10 9 8 7 6 5 4 3 2 1

Library of Congress Cataloging-in-Publication Data has been applied for.

ISBN 978-1-6680-1016-7
ISBN 978-1-6680-1017-4 (ebook)

to the authors who
helped me fall in love
with words:

thank you for sharing
a piece of yourselves
with the world.

contents

this book touches on topics such as anxiety, insecurity, and unhealthy relationships.

changing with the tides

the anchor

to my mind:

we are at war, you and me.
an everlasting exchange of
insults and new wounds
and apologies
that always come just a little too late.

by the time you say
i'm sorry
i have already absorbed the blow.
a new battle scar has risen on my skin.
my body cannot defend itself from you anymore.

and i'm scared a truce will never come.

like an anchor
around my ankles,
i can't escape the voice
in my head that says
you'll never be
anything but nothing.

to insecurity:

if i could step out of my body
and see myself from another view,
would i recognize me?

would i see everything that i think
is so wrong?

(would i see everything that i think
is so unworthy of love?)

i urge my mouth to open
and push the words out.
i have so much to say,
but i choke on

self-doubt.

to anxiety:

every conversation i have
becomes your new favorite song
and you play it on repeat,
only pressing pause
once i've analyzed every word.

(you've made me fear
the sound of my own voice.)

i am sitting on the bus, on my way to the store. the girl
next to me sneezes. i say bless you and she doesn't say
anything back and i wonder if it's because i said it too
quietly or because she thinks i'm weird for talking to a
stranger. the bus slows as it arrives at my stop and i stand
too soon, stumbling to catch myself, praying i won't fall.
i hear two boys laughing and i wonder if they are laughing
at me. i say thank you to the driver and he doesn't say
anything back and i wonder if it's because i said it too
quietly or because he thinks i'm weird for thanking him.
i am walking along the side of the road, on my way to the
store. earbuds in. head down. counting the lines in the
pavement as i walk. i accidentally make eye contact with
a girl passing by so i smile. she doesn't smile back and i
wonder if it's because i smiled too softly or because i am
invisible. (god, i hope i am invisible.)

to the one who keeps letting me down:

i love when you hold me.
feeling your hands wrap around mine.
feeling your hands slowly open.
feeling your hands let me go.

i love the feeling of falling so much
that i keep reaching for you
just so you can let
       me
          go
             again.

you hurt and you lie
and you break me like an
ocean wave
     breaks on
         the shore
and i keep swimming back
because somehow there are still
pieces of me
     that you have
         not destroyed.
you are the ocean's current
pushing me away
and pulling
     me right
         back in
and i am the waves that
foolishly curl around
you and
     refuse to
         let go.

changing with the tides

to the one who watched me fall:

when we first met,
you swept my feet off the ground.
who knew you would be the one
to push me back down?

before i knew it,
my body was caught in quicksand
and the only way out was
the pull of your hand.

but you said you couldn't reach me,
so i sank deeper into the ground
and watched you walk away
while i slowly drowned.

if you were falling,
there is no distance
my arms wouldn't reach
to catch you.

 (i guess i just wasn't
worth saving.)

changing with the tides

to the one who used me:

my bones are weak
from carrying you on my back
for so long.
i sacrificed my strength for you
but now i can no longer
smile without pain

and here you are,
walking just fine,
stronger than ever.

i held my breath
to keep you alive
while you took enough air
for us both to survive.

to the ones who take and take and take:

you are eyes closed
when i want to be seen
and ears shut
when i beg to be heard.
you are arms folded
when i crave to be held
and voice quiet
when i need to be reassured.

it's funny—
i'm always
placing love into your palms
but when it's time to give it back,

suddenly your hands are empty.

changing with the tides

to the one who stole from me:

i offered you pieces of my soul
without a second thought,
as if i was sure you would give them back.
and when you still needed more,
i dug a little deeper,
pulled out my heart like a weed
and planted it carefully in your hands.

and i've learned that
sometimes,
giving everything
means nothing
to the person who
means everything
to you.

(and when i gave you everything,
i was left with nothing.)

i am strong for
giving away my heart
but i am weak for
letting you keep it.

changing with the tides

to the one who lied:

you said you would love me
if i gave you my trust
so i trusted you.
you said you would stay
if i changed myself
so i changed for you.
you said you would come back
if i begged enough times
so i begged for you.

and only after all this
did i ask you to stay,
but you only sighed
and wandered away.

maybe it's easier for me
to swallow lies than to swallow truth.
maybe that's why i never stop
craving the taste of you.

to the one who controlled me:

like the leaves that hang
on autumn trees,
i changed my colors for you
just so i could hear you say
i'm beautiful.

but do you still recognize me
after i made the changes
you asked for?
or am i identical
to everyone else who
wasn't good enough for you?

i changed because
losing myself
was easier than
losing you.

to the one i once called home:

you were meant to feel like home
but now your arms are a cage.
your chest was once my pillow
but now i'd rather turn away.
your voice was once a song
but now your words ring in my ears.
i knew something was wrong
but still i pushed aside my fears.
i never gave up on us
but soon you left me in a blur.

you were meant to feel like home
but now you've found a home with her.

i'm sorry i built
a home out of you
like you were made of clay.
i didn't realize you had
no intention of
inviting me to stay.

to the one i want to forget:

i am a keeper of fingerprints
and a collector of dust,
but i crave to remember
everything you once touched.

my fingers trace over the
glass of shattered picture frames.
i close my eyes and urge myself
to toss them in the flames.

i burn the crumpled letters
that remind me of you,
but i can't seem to forget that
you once touched me, too.

*(if only i could burn you
from my skin.)*

loneliness slips past my lips
and settles into my lungs.
the air i used to breathe so peacefully
now feels foreign in my chest.
it doesn't feel safe anymore.

it doesn't feel like you.

to my weakness:

loving you was a game of tug-of-war.
pulling each other in opposite directions
and demanding change
that did not want to come.

so neither of us ever won.
the rope finally tore and
we fell on our backs,
farther apart than where we started.

you always said we were so alike.
everything you did, i wanted to do.

so when you put the blame on me,
naturally, i blamed myself, too.

to the one who broke me:

did you feel my heart shatter
when you crushed it with your
bare hands?
did you pull the pieces
from your skin like broken glass,
or did you keep them
as a reminder,
a trophy,
of how you hurt me?

my favorite game is the one
where you try to heal me
and we both pretend you are
not the reason i am broken
in the first place.

to the one who always wins:

your legs are much longer than mine
but still i chase your footprints on the shore,
and it doesn't matter how many steps i take
because you're always ahead.
i'll never catch up.
i'll never be good enough.
i'm just a shadow lurking behind you,
hoping one day you'll turn around
and notice how i long to be by your side.

i am the master of silent suffering—
no one can see through my somber smile.
like a crab in the sand,
i burrow into my sadness and
settle in like it's my home.

no one ever seems to notice
i'm underground.

to my dark cloud:

i gazed up at the sky and saw
cryptic, mysterious, powerful.
always protecting me.
(always following me.)

you were a thunderstorm
when the sky was clear
and i chased sidewalks to
escape the rain,

shielded my ears
from the sting of thunder,
cowered under roofs to avoid
the lightning you threw.

oh, how i wanted to be the sunlight
that swallowed your darkness.
how i wanted to be the rainbow
after your storm.

i am strong, but
i cannot stop fury
with my bare hands.

she surrendered herself
to the darkness
because she grew so tired
of waiting
for the sun to rise.

to the one i pushed away:

when it rained today,
i thought of you,
a little more than
i usually do.
and i wished as waterdrops
settled onto my skin
that i could go back in time
and just let you in.

i was only trying
to water your roots
so you could grow.

i did not intend to
drown you.

(forgive me.)

to the one who doesn't need me anymore:

suddenly, you fell in love with the sun,
bowing gently toward the light,
seeking the warmth
you used to ask from me.

you only grew strong from
the water i gave you to drink,
but it wasn't long before you
stabbed me with your thorns.

i am both a healer
and a harmer.
i fix everyone i can
but in the end,
i have no strength left
to heal myself.

to the one who is always on my mind:

i miss you most during storms,
when the wind sweeps through my head
and scavenges for the memories of you that
i had carefully placed into cobwebbed corners.

i miss you most during storms,
when the rain seeps into my skin
and leaves me yearning for the body
that once kept me safe and warm.

i miss you most during storms,
but if i'm being honest,
i miss you always.
because i thought

you would be here always.

my arms search for you in the night,
desperately grasping at air.

meanwhile in my dreams,
i reach for your hand and you are there.

changing with the tides

to my enemy:

how bravely you stood across from me
when you didn't stand a chance.
we raised our swords defiantly
for our battle to commence.
i knew all of your weaknesses
and defeated you with glee
but when you removed your helmet
my reflection stared back at me.

if i write down
all the vicious words
i use
to describe myself
and set fire to the pages,
will they cease to exist?

(i can't think of another
way to escape.)

to the person i was yesterday:

i believe in change,
the change that people don't often notice
until it's already happened
like
petals wilting,
   eyes reddening,
     raindrops evaporating.

i believe in change
that is slow and careful,
patiently lingering
like
flowers blooming,
   pearls forming,
     hearts healing.

i see little hints of you
tucked in my reflection
and i wonder if you'd be proud of me.

(i wonder if you'd forgive me for all
the things i used to say about you.)

i stepped cautiously in front of my mirror to find a girl
with swollen eyes dressed in armor, protecting her body
from the sting of the words i had been throwing at her for
years. i didn't realize how much damage i caused until i
saw her dented shield and trembling arms. but she never
surrendered, never threw her shield down in defeat.
in her, i saw resilience. a girl waiting patiently for change.

i'm sorry, i pleaded.
can you forgive me?

the sail

to anxiety, ii:

you've always been good at
choking me
with my own words

but

i am
tired of feeling tired
when i speak.

today
i must apologize to myself
for placing a hand
over my mouth
while my voice patiently
waited to be heard.

(*i'm sorry.*)

changing with the tides

to the one who hurt me:

when i was nine, my brother and i
caught a frog and kept it in a bucket outside,
hidden away in the tree house our dad built for us.
after school, we searched through the grass
for bugs for it to eat and
filled a bowl with water for it to drink and bathe.
through four cold winter months,
the frog had no shelter beyond the leaves
that blew in from the branches above.

when i look back, i realize how it suffered.
i realize the pain we caused
even though we had good intentions.
we were just loving it the best way we knew how.

so when you look back, i hope you realize
i suffered, too.
how the love you draped over me wore a disguise.
it looked like water to drink but really
it drowned me.
it looked like food to eat but really
it starved me.
it looked like shelter from the cold but really
i felt so far from home.

what i'm trying to say is, i know you had good
intentions. but you just weren't any good for me.

i hope one day
you realize that
love is not
synonymous
with pain.

to the one who stole from me, ii:

(you made me forget i am human.)
i gave you my happiness by the handful,
harvesting pieces of myself as if i were
plucking petals from daisies.
(you told me i couldn't survive without you.)
i thought you were my water, my ray of light,
but you were a drought, an eternal night.
(you told me i had too much love to give.)
i was a field of blooming flowers,
but you tore every stem from their roots
and left me with a barren body.
(you made me forget i need love, too.)

now i am regrowing my garden
and keeping these flowers for myself.
(you will never pull the life from me again.)

you washed over me
like a wave of darkness
and still expected me to
light the sky for you.

to the one who lied, ii:

i am not afraid
to empty
the world of you
and bury your
broken promises
with ash.

(so watch me burn
all the pages
i ever dared to
write your name.)

do not weep for me.
you are not worthy of
my tongue speaking your name,
my skin knowing your touch,
my mind swimming in memories of you.

do not weep for me.
don't you dare shed a tear.
because i am done weeping for you.

to the one who held me back:

my ankles burn from the rope
that you've tied around them

but i haven't stopped walking,
have i?

this is what happens when you tell me
i'm not good enough.

(i prove you wrong.)

i was born with an
everlasting flame
within me
and the fire only
grows stronger
every time you try to
extinguish my spark.

(be careful not to get burned.)

to the one i fear:

the words on your tongue
only escape when they are angry,
spewing rage and spite.
but when they land
on my skin
they turn to joy
because if i let them
collect like dust,
maybe i'll never have the courage
to shake them off.
maybe i'll become angry like you,
and i don't want to be.
i want to be happy.

i will be happy.

happiness lives
in a little room in my heart
and some days it
prefers the curtains drawn shut.

(and i've learned that's okay.)

to the one who gave up on me:

~~i'm sorry i~~
~~disappointed you.~~

farewell.

when you left, my heart was broken.
i felt pain like a thousand knives and
i cried a thousand tears and
i wrote a thousand poems about you.
i'm not telling you this
to make you feel guilty or
to make you come back.
i'm telling you this because i'm healing,
and i'm doing it on my own.
you left because you thought i was weak,
but your absence made me strong.
like it or not, you've changed me for the better.
so i thank you.

to the one i can't forget:

my body needs a reminder that you're gone
so i embrace the cold with open arms.
my teeth chatter.
my body shivers.
goosebumps crawl across my skin.
i softly exhale the unfinished memories that
i forgot to push out of my lungs,
the ones that have been weighing me down
for months,
though it feels like centuries.
they sit like tiny clouds
in the air before vanishing completely.
(would you believe my chest already feels lighter?
it turns out my body loves emptiness
almost as much as it loves carrying your burdens.)

i embrace the cold with open arms
because i don't want to remember your warmth.

i don't want to remember what you took from me.

i can't erase you from my mind
but maybe i can scrub you from my skin
so i turn my face to the sky
and let the rain sink in.
water slides down my cheeks
and falls softly to the ground.
i pretend the rain is cleansing me
from the hands that held me down.
the storm slowly stops
and the sky returns to blue.
i have rid my body of your grip—

i am completely untouched by you.

to the one who walked away:

i was scared to be without you.
you used to breathe life into my lungs—
then suddenly i had to breathe on my own.

but i've learned i can exist happily
without you.

actually, i can flourish
without you.

what a relief it was to
let you go
and remember how it feels to
thrive on my own.

to irony:

when he left
he thought i would be alone

but when he left
i found myself again.

on days i feel lonely
i remember all the people
i let go of because i knew
what was best for me.

and i feel a little less alone
knowing that if no one else has my back,
at least i do.

to the one i envy:

i pretend you're perfect,
though recently
i discovered
you're not.

you see, i have spent so
much time wanting to be you
that it hurts to say
i've changed my mind.

(because there are
pieces of me
that i would
really miss.)

i change with the tides.
sometimes i am big, fierce,
towering over the sea,
destroying castles,
carving pearls from sand.
sometimes i am small, gentle,
rippling across shorelines,
curling around ankles,
sinking between toes.

i change with the tides.
i am learning to love
all the shapes of me.

to writing:

you strengthen me
even when i am
telling the story of someone
who weakened me.

i wrote through the pain
until the ink ran dry and
finally i saw happiness
on the other side.

(writing heals me.)

to healing:

just when i thought i never would,
i woke up and felt a little less pain.
i walked a little faster,
stood a little taller,
smiled a little wider.

just when i thought i never could,
i put myself back together.

i chase storms
without fear because
i know the
dark clouds
will eventually lead to
blue skies.

to sadness:

the sand swallowed me whole one day,
and for a while i was sinking.
i fought the earth,
pulling my body up
with all of my strength,
though i sank deeper still.

my body became a seed one day,
and my mind became water.
i was both the healer and the survivor.
and i grew.
it took days, weeks, months
but slowly i grew.

light pierced the ground one day,
and i could finally see beyond the darkness
that had become my home.
i could finally see how much i had grown.

i emerged from the rigid sand and
sunrays pressed kisses on my cheeks,
and i smiled.

(i defeated you.)

she pulled herself
from the darkness
because she saw
a sliver of sunrise
and it reminded her
of the warm days.

to sadness, ii:

for the first time in a long time,
i am excited for dawn to break—
to feel the earth wake beneath my feet,
to watch the moon yawn and slowly fall asleep.

of course, i'd be silly to think
you're gone forever,
that you'll never
come knocking at my door again—
but the last time you showed up,
i didn't believe i could defeat you.

this time, i know i can.

one morning
you will open your eyes
and know it will be a good day
without having prayed for it
the night before.

to tomorrow:

i used to think of each day
as a fire i needed to smother,
a task on a list i needed to complete.

now i think of myself as the flame,
unable to be extinguished,
leaving behind a trail of ash wherever i go.

(i'm here,
and i'm not going anywhere.)

if the sun can wake up
every morning and
warm the earth,
so can
i.

to new beginnings:

you can close this chapter
of your life and never look back
or you can flip through the pages,
revisit old memories,
reflect on how different you once were.

that's the magic of
writing your own story—
you'll meet new characters,
travel to new places,
face new obstacles,
and the best part:

deciding how to overcome them
and then realizing
you can.

don't just watch the world
as it spins around you.
uncover it.
peel back each layer and really look.
do you see?
the world wants to show you its secrets
if you let it.

(there is so much to look forward to.
please don't give up.)

to mourning:

i feel you at the most random moments,
like you are waiting for me
to be happy again before you
hit me with another wave and
knock me to the ground.

i feel you when i am
surrounded by people
and when i am alone,
when i am wide awake
and drifting to sleep.

i know you'll never truly fade,
and i've learned that's okay
because you help me remember
people worth remembering.

(thank you for giving me the time
i need to heal.)

i'd like to think the stars in the sky
needed you more up there than i needed you
down here.

(i'll think that even if it's not true.
because you're not here and i need you.)

so if i'm going to be without you for the rest
of my days, then i'd like to think you're
lighting the sky for eternity.

(i see you in every sunrise.
i'd recognize your glow anywhere.)

to the horizon:

you are the calm
that takes breaths away.
when the waves are crashing
and the wind is roaring
you are inexplicably silent,

holding the sky above your head
and never complaining about
the heaviness in your bones.

you underestimate the strength
it takes to be delicate,

to bare your soul
like a rose eager to bloom,

to sacrifice your petals
as they wilt and fall.

do not mistake
fragility for weakness.

your stem can withstand
even the strongest of winds.

to survivors:

when the ground below you
erupted in flames,
you walked barefoot,
braving the pain.

no matter what you've been through,
the pain that you've endured,
i will believe your story,
of this you can be sure.

(i can't take the pain away,
but i will listen.)

to the perfectionists:

there is not a soul on this earth that is perfect.
there are no feet that have not stumbled
and no eyes that have not cried.
there are no lights that have not flickered
and no flowers that have not dried.

there is not a soul on this earth that is perfect.
(please don't be so hard on yourself.)

be still. breathe.
the earth will continue to spin
even if you are not pushing it.

to the ones who give
and give and give:

do you remember the laughter?
the fluttering deep in your chest?
like a tiny robin flapping its wings
and settling in its nest?

that's just what you do, it seems—
make your body a home for all.
but once they've used your wings for warmth,
you stand a little less tall.

maybe it's time to fly alone,
let your wings reach new heights.
(if others keep holding you back,
how will you see all the sights?)

instead of lowering
my expectations so
i wouldn't get hurt,
i raised them to what i
have always deserved.

to setbacks:

you trusted me when i
didn't trust myself and
you caught me
before i ever fell.
looking back,
i thought i made it
here on my own.

now i realize you
are the reason i've grown.

i have been held down by anchors
and swallowed by waves.
i have tumbled along the ocean floor
and swam miles in total darkness.
i have prayed for light to guide my eyes
or a song to guide my ears
and when neither came,
i relied on the beat of my heart
and it told me exactly where i
needed to go.

to the ones afraid to flourish:

like a blooming flower
in a field of buds,
you cannot be
afraid to grow
just because
the others won't.

the moon watched
silently as she stood
on her tiptoes
and carefully
plucked a star from the night sky.
she didn't take the
brightest one or the biggest one—
no—
she chose the star
farthest from reach.
she was
tired of being told
she could never make it.
and now she carries the
proof in her pocket.

(but she'll never show them—
no—
it's a secret between
her and the moon.)

to the silencers:

you cannot quiet our hunger—
our passion—
for change.
and no matter where you hide,
highest mountaintop
or lowest valley,
you will hear the echo of our roars.

(we aren't going anywhere.)

the earth is loud.
don't you hear it begging for us to listen?
every clap of thunder,
every howl of wind,
every crash of water.
this is the earth asking for protection.

(and time is running out.)

to the quiet ones
who are afraid
of the sound of
their own voices:

write
and your words will
scream from the page.
(and you will be heard.)

my voice survived a drought
when my confidence was weak.

meanwhile, pages drowned with
the words i couldn't speak.

(writing is my safety.)

to the ones with their
heads in the clouds:

never let anyone
pull
you

down.

(they're just jealous
of your view.)

carve the earth from clay
and hold it lightly in your palm.
pull a star from your pocket
and skip it like a stone.

don't listen when they say rivers can't be
painted gold and islands can't be white.
you see, the world is yours to imagine
if you simply close your eyes.

to life's purpose:

there is nothing more powerful than you.
you hold the key to the universe
and choose not to share what's behind the door.
you are the fuel that powers sleepless nights
and the unanswered question on everyone's mind.

maybe one day you will reveal the answer,
but i prefer not knowing.

i prefer to wonder.

i whisper my wishes to the sky
and watch the stars grow bright.
maybe the earth is listening
when i speak my dreams into the night.

to the future:

we are servants to the unexplored,
living each day for you
without knowing
what you will give
in return.

but i am not afraid of you.
from now on,
i will embrace each day
with open arms because i have
so much love in my heart

and i can't bear to
leave this earth
before i've had
the chance
to share it.

you were radiant
long before the first sunray
landed upon your skin.
you are radiant because of
the glow you emit,
and though you feel like
only one person,
the world would be dimmer
without you in it.

changing with the tides

to the ones who underestimate themselves:

when you finally break the anchor
and remember how it feels to be free,
you will look back and ask
how you ever doubted yourself
when all along
you carried the strength
in your own two palms.

i lost who i was,
forgot myself in the hands of someone
who didn't know how to treat me.
i'm slowly undoing their devastation,
unfolding my corners and picking up the pieces
that were chiseled away.

i lost who i was,
or maybe a better word is misplaced.
because i found myself again
and this time—
like a glistening shell found
hidden in the sand—
i am placing myself
in my hands
and never letting go.

to the ones with regrets:

our mistakes shape us.
so we must learn to
embrace them
because they are reminders of
who we were,
who we are,
and who we can be.

i am a ghost
haunting my own home,
swallowing the dust
on old photo frames and books
just to get a taste of who i once was.

although broken,
the mirror i used to look into
hangs crooked on the walls
and i remember all the hours
i spent picking myself apart.

for old times' sake, i stand in
front of the mirror one last time
and see nothing.

invisible like i had always wanted.

but now, i wish i could see
my soft blue eyes that i always
thought were too light,
my hair that was too thick,
my smile that was too wide.

i wish i could see all the
flaws i used to hate
so i could show them love.

to the one who controlled me, ii:

yes,
i regret letting you change me.
but i do not regret having the chance
to be someone else
because in that short time
i learned that i missed
who i really am.

you cannot simply
pick the pieces of me
that you want and
give the rest back.

i am not yours to
edit
alter
tailor
manipulate
until i am perfect in your eyes.

(i never will be.)

to society:

my whole life i've cared too much
what you thought of me
but now i don't care at all.
maybe you look at me—
at my dark eyes and unkempt hair—
and see tired. broken. fragile.

but i look below the surface
and see strong. brave. compassionate.

(maybe one day
you'll look below the surface, too.)

in this world,
there is no reassuring voice that says
you're beautiful
when you peer in the water
at your reflection.

you have to say it yourself.

and while you're there,
remind yourself that
your mind is smart,
your heart is strong,
your life is valuable,
and your voice needs to be heard.

 (be your own magic mirror.)

to the person i am today:

i promise i will start loving you again.
i just need to remember
how it feels to be proud of you,
to look in the mirror and be in awe of you.

i just need to remember what it was like
before i told you
you weren't good enough.

i buried you alive, piling
doubt and loathing
onto your body like soil,

so only i can bring you back to life.

(and i will.
i promise.)

she lowered her arms,
dropping her shield to the floor
with a crash.

i forgive you, she whispered.

connect with shelby:

instagram: @shelbyleighpoetry

tiktok: @shelbyleighpoetry

twitter: @shelbyleighpoet

learn more at shelbyleigh.co.